Best wishes

From the author

Eve Simpson

Aberdour and Burntisland in old picture postcards

by
Eric Simpson

European Library – Zaltbommel/Netherlands

The author:

Eric Simpson, a former Head of History at Moray House College in Edinburgh, is now a free-lance lecturer and writer. Born and brought up in Buckie, Banffshire, he has lived in Dalgety Bay since 1966. His publications include 'The Auld Grey Toun – Dunfermline in the time of Andrew Carnegie 1835-1919', 'Dalgety – the story of a parish', 'Discovering Banff, Moray & Nairn' (John Donald) and two other books in the European Library series, namely 'Dunfermline and Rosyth in old picture postcards' (with George Robertson) and 'Inverkeithing and Dalgety in old picture postcards' (with George Hastie).

Acknowledgements:

Many people have helped in one way or another, but special thanks are due to the following: Alan Barker, George Robertson, John Taylor, Jennifer and Morrice McCrae, Mrs. Christina Pont, Mrs. Cathy King, Mrs. Isobel Low, Mrs. Vallance, Ian Somerville, Edward A. Wilson, Mrs. Edith May, Thomas Milne, Chris Neale and staff of Dunfermline District Library. Thanks must be given also to the Royal Commission on the Ancient & Historical Monuments of Scotland for permission to reproduce photographs 15 and 28 and to the Scottish Record Office for photograph 50.

As ever, I am exceedingly indebted to my son Fraser for photographic assistance and to my wife Kathleen for her patience, proof-reading skills and other indispensable forms of support.

Cover picture:

The postcard, which was selected for the cover picture, shows Shore Road, Aberdour, around 1900. The donkey was possibly a stuffed one, perhaps one of the props from a nearby photographer's studio.

GB ISBN 90 288 5754 0 / CIP

INTRODUCTION

Aberdour and Burntisland are communities, each with its own distinctive history and appearance. They have, nevertheless, a great deal in common. For a start, they both have an imposing-looking castle. While Aberdour Castle is a carefully-preserved, ancient monument, Burntisland's Rossend, though threatened with demolition, was purchased in 1975 and restored to purposeful use by a local architectural firm. Both communities can boast, too, that they have an historic and architecturally interesting kirk. Aberdour has an ancient Norman-style parish church, St. Fillan's, which was discarded and its roof removed in 1796, but, thanks to munificent gifts, was restored and rededicated in 1926. In contrast to St. Fillan's, with its typically medieval layout, Burntisland's late 16th century parish kirk was designed to facilitate the 'preaching of the Word'. Here the pulpit replaced the altar as the focus of attention. The fine 17th and 18th century craft symbols and other painted panels on the sailors' loft testify to the importance of the burgh's seafarers to both kirk and community. It was, incidentally, at a General Assembly held at the Burntisland kirk, that James VI took the first steps that led to the making of the new translation of the Bible – the Authorized Version.

As numerous tombstones in the kirkyard show, Aberdour too had its seafarers, who played a vital role in the life of the village. Its attractive old harbour was once used for shipping coal and other minerals. Until around 1870, coal-carts were a common sight as they rumbled through the streets, via Park Lane (then Coal Wynd) and Shore Road, heading for the sailing colliers, tied up at the quay. Burntisland's harbour is obviously much larger and was always more important. As a port, Burntisland reached its apogee in the 19th and early 20th centuries, when very large quantities of coal were despatched there by rail for export to the rest of Britain and continental Europe. In 1913 over 2,400,000 tons of coal passed through the port. While its coal traffic and most of its former general trade has gone, large quantities of bauxite are landed for the use of the sizeable ALCAN alumina works at Burntisland. The need, at that time, for large quantities of coal and also an abundance of water, helped to explain why the then British Aluminium Company opted for Burntisland.

Where ports exist, boat-building is an obvious associated industry. Over the years, quite a few small craft have been constructed at Aberdour, most recently at a small yard at the Ha' Craig, or Hawk Craig as it is erroneously known. Ship-building became at Burntisland, though, an important local industry. During the Second World War the vessels constructed at Burntisland included a number of merchant aircraft-carriers, ships that played a vital role in protecting British convoys and thus helped to defeat the German U-boat menace. It may be added that earlier, when enemy submarines began to threaten the British fleet and merchant navy during the First World War, an experimental research station was established at Ha' Craig, close by the popular Silver Sands beach. Top scientists were brought to Aberdour to help develop hydrophones for underwater detection purposes. Although ship-building as such came to an end at Burntisland, the yard was subsequently developed for the construction of modules and other structures for the North Sea oil and gas industries. Consafe (Burntisland) Ltd. are the present occupiers of the fabrication yard.

Both Aberdour and Burntisland were ferry ports, with the latter easily the more important of the two. When Burntisland became, in 1847, the railhead for Fife for the Edinburgh and Northern Railway Company, that town rapidly developed into the premier ferry port on the north side of the Forth. Indeed, three years later the world's first roll-on roll-off railway ferry was established for transporting coal from Burntisland to Granton on the other side of the Forth. The ferrying of coal across the Forth came to an end when the Forth Railway Bridge was completed in 1890. Passenger services continued on a greatly reduced basis until the Second World War. In the early 1950s, an attempt to introduce a car and passenger ferry service, utilising converted wartime tank-landing craft, was a financial failure. In 1991 an attempt was made to restore a passenger-carrying service to this historic route, but the service, while attractive to holiday-makers, failed to attract the requisite number of regular commuters.

During the 19th and early 20th centuries, passenger-carrying steamers, as many old postcards testify, were vital factors in the growth of the holiday trade. The people of both Burntisland and Aberdour utilised their natural advantages – good bathing beaches and an attractive and accessible location – to sell their communities as sea-bathing resorts. Both towns were served by paddle-steamer fleets, bearing excursionists and other holiday-makers from Edinburgh's ports – Leith, Newhaven and Granton. In the 1890s, in the height of summer there were up to 9 sailings a day from Leith to Aberdour. Later, the opening of the Forth Railway Bridge brought increased numbers of visitors from Glasgow and the industrial west, and Aberdour was placed on the railway map for the first time. Its railway station, which has won awards for floral displays, dates from that period. For Burntisland, improved railway communication with the west was welcomed as part compensation for the loss, post-1890, of most of its ferry-borne trade and traffic. Another blow that struck Burntisland at that time was the final closure, in 1893, of the Binnend Oil Works, a firm whose workforce at its peak numbered close to 1,000 (see illustration 75). The main railway line to Edinburgh and to points east and north still survives though and forms a prime asset for both communities.

Although the long-stay holidaymakers of former years are no more, both Aberdour and Burntisland see many visitors, especially day-trippers, attracted to the tourist facilities at Aberdour's Silver Sands and Burntisland's links and adjacent beach. The houses and lodgings that were once let to summer visitors, now house permanent residents, drawn to these coastal communities by the self-same amenities that made Aberdour and Burntisland favourite places of resort in the pioneering days of popular tourism.

1. Countless visitors arrived at Aberdour by paddle-steamers from Leith. Here we see the Galloway Saloon Steam Packet Company's 'Lord Morton' at Aberdour Stone Pier. Converted into a hospital ship during the First World War, this steamer was scuttled in the Russian White Sea in 1919, to keep her from falling into Bolshevik hands. Notice the changing boxes on the left side of the postcard. They were removed in 1930 and new huts built.

2. As the 'Lord Morton' departs, crowds line the harbour wall to watch the annual Aberdour Regatta (the oldest in the Forth). Rowing boats, hired out by the hour, were another popular attraction. On the Ha' Craig across the harbour, we see, marked with a cross, the Temperance Hotel (now the Forth View Hotel), built beside the 'New Pier'. When tides were too low for the Stone Pier to be used, steamers headed instead for the Ha' Craig pier. The single-funnelled steamer was one of the Galloway ships that were fitted with a folding mast and telescopic funnel, to enable them to sail under the railway bridge at Alloa.

3. Since the lease for the new pier prohibited the landing of passengers on Sundays, large rowing boats, like the one on the beach, were used to ferry passengers ashore. The building that is now the Forth View Hotel was built in 1881 as a family home by Leith entrepreneur, M.P. Galloway. When Galloway sold the cheerfully named Bleak House, it was converted into a hotel. According to a 1908 advert, the Temperance Hotel or the Hydro, as it was variously called, was 'the only House with Sea Water Baths on the Firth of Forth'. Pierrots used to perform on the grass beside the hotel.

4. Another Galloway paddle-steamer has disembarked its passengers at the Ha' Craig pier. 'The Wood Pier', as the title on this card puts it, was built in 1866 by Donald R. MacGregor, a Leith shipowner. Excursionists, in their 'Sunday suits' and best dresses, are heading away from the pier, passing on their way a shop, selling 'Ice Cream & Refreshments'. The Forth View Hotel (left) is seen here from the rear.

5. When tides allowed, passengers landed at the old Stone Pier and then walked, like the Edwardian-period visitors, along the promenade. In the distance we see the cottage, which was erected in 1817 and was the first house to be built at the shore. In the inter-war years, the promenade was still a place to see and to be seen. Notice that iron railings had replaced the former ramshackle wooden ones. On the grass, near where the pierrots used to play, a uniformed band is performing.

6. Seabank House, the second oldest of the shore-facing dwellings, was built as a 'Marine Villa' (and dower-house) for the Hendersons of Fordell. Later it became a hydro, but in May 1912, when this card was posted, it was classified as a hotel. 'It is quiet at present,' wrote the sender, 'but woe when the trippers come.' In the early 1900s, deckchairs were not yet part of the seaside scene. Someone, though, has taken a folding chair down onto the sands. This photo was evidently taken on a day when the trippers were absent.

7. In this circa 1930 photograph of the West Beach we see no fewer than 5 motor-launches: 1/- was the charge for a trip to Inchcolm. By then, too, deckchairs were available for hire on the beach, as the board with price-list and the stack of deckchairs clearly show. The alternative name for the West Beach was the Black Sands, which possibly dates back to the time when coal was shipped from the Stone Pier. In the 1950s, regular dookers using the changing boxes, enjoyed Mrs. Wotherspoon's inimitable brand of tea. Only the foundations remain to show where the bathing boxes stood.

8. With many tourists going to and from the piers, Shore Road was a good location for a street-trader and also for pubs and eating-places. John McLauchlan's Star Hotel (now the Cedar Inn) can be seen on the far left. Kinnaird's Tea Garden (see cover picture also) stood opposite. Inside and out, and up aloft in the roof garden, this was an ornately-adorned building. Hammocks were slung from the roof inside, to house visitors seeking basic accommodation. After the First World War, when it was a Forces' canteen, it became the Institute, serving as a public hall, but also housing 'gentlemen boarders'.

9. As in the cover photograph, Shore Road is viewed from the north. It is the same donkey, possibly a stuffed one from the collection of props in Claude Low's photographic studio, which is the ornately-gabled building on the right. Notice the number of placards adorning Kinnaird's Tea Gardens. Observe too the ghost-like figure on the roof. As well as being a popular destination for visitors, many locals went there for their weekly bath, few houses possessing a bathroom. Now the Aberdour Community Leisure Centre occupies the site.

10. The customers here are enjoying their tea and ginger beer in Milner's Tea Garden, which was located, we are told, off the High Street (on the south side behind the former Cooperative store). As well as purveying teas and ginger beer, J. Milner, who was also a stationer, evidently did a good trade in picture postcards. Observe the pictorial advertisements and what seems to be a rack for pipes.

11. Turning the corner into the High Street, we see that the shop of Niven, the butcher, had a different roof-line then. This Edwardian-period photograph was taken on a winter's day, so there are not many visitors. The 'scholars' from the school round the corner, were only too ready to pose for the photographer. Observe the horsedung on the street, inescapable in those days.

12. Now we are into summer, so in this circa 1909 photograph the striped sunshades are up. As with the previous postcard, the Dr. Spence Memorial Clock is not visible. It was not moved from its original location, fronting the church hall, until the erection of the War Memorial in 1919. The girl, with sunhat and tight-waisted skirt in the left-hand corner, is Harriet Comfort, who was a telegraph messenger and then Post Office clerkess before emigrating to Canada.

13. We see the same area, taken from the opposite direction, with Seath's Golf Restaurant prominent on the right. Rather incredibly, the restaurant could cater for 300 at one sitting. A later circa 1920 advert boasted that the premises could provide shelter for 600 and that 'Schools & Public Works' were contracted for. The building to the east of the restaurant was W. Crow the plumber's premises. Notice the cobbled gutter and the absence of any pavement on the left side of the road.

14. Passing to the interwar years, we see that the buildings on the left side of the road have been radically changed. Craven A cigarettes, Selo and Ensign films, and radios are now on sale in what was latterly Milburn's shop. A further indication of changing standards is the presence, further along the High Street, of a Hot Water Engineer. Observe the milk-churns on the delivery-cart and on the new pavement. In the distance we see the Free Kirk, later St. Colme's. It was demolished in 1964 and new dwellings were erected on this Sands Place site.

15. There are very few photographs of the Livingston Lane corner, an area which is greatly changed. The notice on the left, pointing to J. Hamilton's Dairy down the lane, states that cycles could be stored there. Immediately to the right the notice simply reads, 'D. Philip, Coal Merchant.' Rather curiously, another coal merchant, J. Barclay, resided next door. At that time, probably circa 1930, the bakery next door was owned by Thomas Milne. His specialities were shortbread and gingerbread.

16. An older version of the baker's premises, then just a two-storey building, can be seen in this picture. The old Primary School with schoolhouse next door, is on the right. The girls wear pinnies to protect their frocks. This school continued in use until 1967. The writer's daughter was one of the last batch of pupils to enroll in the infant class in that year.

17. Forestairs, cobbled gutters, apartments to let signs and lamps, bracketed to house-walls were features of the Edwardian High Street. The street-lamps were then oil-fired. Gas mains were laid in 1914. Next to McLean's Aberdour Hotel, there is a railing. The restaurant extension had not then been built. This postcard predates the Dr. Spence Memorial. Notice though the ivy-laden kirkyard wall.

18. The Dr. Spence Memorial Clock (1910) is seen here in its original location. (Incidentally there are two memorials to the well-regarded Dr. Spence in Burntisland also.) The kirkyard gate was on the west side near The Pharmacy. The top photograph is actually a typical John Valentine forgery. Most of the figures supposedly walking up the street have been added, probably to update the picture. The boys on the extreme right, who were from the Crow family, were, however, in the original genuine photograph, which we see below.

19. In this mid-1920s view, the clock has gone and the wall has been lowered to give due prominence to the War Memorial commemorating the slain of the First World War. The use of motor-buses, both on regular services and for pleasure trips, greatly increased after the war. The postcards on display outside The Pharmacy (now J. Taylor's) would have been W.T. Inkster's own brand. In the 1920s, the chemist also sold golf clubs and balls and 'High-class Tobaccos & Cigarettes'. Notice that the railings, where the restaurant is sited, have been removed.

20. This view of T. McLean's Aberdour Hotel was taken in 1903 and shows the hotel's coachman, a Mr. Finlayson, riding bareback. As the notice indicates, the hotel had its own posting and livery stables, which meant that their horse and vehicle were available for hire and that horses could also be fed and stabled. The entrance to the bar has been moved since then. McLean bottled on the premises Jeffrey's India Pale Ale, brewed at the Heriot Brewery in Edinburgh.

21. Next door to the hotel we see a 1904 view of Harry Mitchell's shop. A relative was on the 'below the stairs' staff at nearby Otterston House, here seen in a 1903 photograph. The front row comprises, from left to right, the housekeeper, parlour maid and valet; in the rear are 'Tweeny' maid, cook and lady's maid. Provision merchants like Harry Mitchell would have been eager to secure the big house's custom.

22. When this photograph was taken, the Post Office was located next door to the Woodside Hotel. Opposite the hotel are the Donibristle gates, which gave access to another of the big houses of the neighbourhood. (For more pictures of Donibristle, Otterston and other country-estates, see the book on Inverkeithing and Dalgety in this series.)

23. The Post Office has now gone and the Woodside Hotel has been extended. The Doune Hall (1913), which is now incorporated in the hotel, had yet to be built. Notice the Woodside Garage in the second picture (an advertisement card) and the opulent-looking limousine strategically placed outside the hotel. Advertisements of the early 1920s, boasted that the hotel possessed an adjoining, up-to-date dance hall (under hotel management), electric light, a large garage, all motor accessories, and cars for hire.

24. Manse Street and Seaside Place were part of the 'New Town', which was built on land feued from the Earl of Morton. As elsewhere, we see many 'To Let' signs and old-style lamp-posts. We see in Seaside Place two 1930s-period cars and gowfers heading for the golf course. During the Second World War, View Forth, on the extreme left, housed high-ranking naval officers. Since Corriemar on the seafront (reached by a garden path) was, for a time, a naval headquarters, this was a convenient abode for them.

25. The 'Old Town', as Easter Aberdour was once aptly named, housed some historic dwellings. Sadly, forestairs and cast-iron lamp standards are no longer to be seen on Main Street. The dwellings with the forestairs, on the left, were removed prior to 1933. When some of the buildings in the middle distance were removed, a new point of access to Murrell Road was constructed. The old road to The Murrell went via Murrell Terrace and Road.

26. The 17th century dwelling on the extreme right (the one with the corbie-stepped gable) was another building that was regrettably demolished. A modern house (10 Main Street) now occupies the site. The sender of this card, writing in April 1919, was 'delighted with everything'. For her, as with quite a number of other visitors, one of the major attractions was the 'heaps of lovely walks about here'.

27. The name 'Glebe' indicates that these were former church lands. The houses on the west side were constructed in the 1920s. It is said that some of the construction timbers came from the old limestone mine at Nine Lums. The card was published by local chemist, W.T. Inkster, who was the Aberdour chemist from 1923 until 1970.

28. Contrasts in dress are apparent in this circa 1930 photograph. The girls outside Bald's grocery store, on Silver Sands Terrace, are clad in light summer dresses, whereas the older gents beside the Station Inn (now Drift Inn) are more soberly dressed. Observe the shop's rough-and-ready sunshade and the tin-panel advertisements on the walls. The inn's iron railings and the lamp standard (note the glass has been removed) have not survived.

29. Aberdour Castle and doocot appear on the left, and part of Easter Aberdour on the right, in this circa 1900 view. Home Park (originally Cow Park) then consisted of two divided villas and a cottage. In 1871, a Leith building firm feued this field from the Earl of Morton. Their speculation failed, so the bowling green and croquet lawn, which were to be part of the scheme, remained projects on paper.

30. The nearby Silver Sands (formerly the White Sands) were a perennial attraction, although this photograph was taken on a quiet day. This 1930s view, from the era of blazers and one-piece swimsuits, is a J.B. White of Dundee card. 'Having a day at the Seaside', wrote one correspondent in August 1906, 'but oh dear! the Edinburgh crowds!!' The message on another postcard from that era reads: 'Far better on those sands than at church on Sunday.'

31. After the opening, in 1890, of the North British Railway Company's new station, picnic parties and trippers came to Aberdour in even larger numbers and from further afield. The Aberdour railway staff (and in Edwardian days there were many of them) are looking at the photographer rather than at the incoming train.

32. This Dunfermline family group arrived on a day trip – a day at Aberdour beach being a last holiday treat for the bairns before returning to school. Going by bus from Dunfermline to Aberdour in 1928, was regarded by the children as like going to the ends of the earth.

The Aberdour "Al Fresco" Entertainers, 1905
Valentines Series 48050

33. In the early 1900s, a number of different concert parties entertained the visitors at the West Sands each summer season. One troupe at least, who played at the shore in the summer of 1900, came from 'the other side of the border'. The 'Al Fresco' entertainers were just one of the many groups who performed at Aberdour in the summer season. The sender of this card (1905) had enjoyed listening to the minstrels and further remarked that there were 'a great many Leith folk here'.

34. While some groups of pierrots had the benefit of a canvas-topped stage, others used only a simple platform. Notice that the audience here had to find their own seats. With no enclosed space, the performers had to be good at 'bottling', i.e. cajoling cash from the customers. When the weather was bad, the pierrots played in a nearby hall. It was 'the fair sex', one newspaper correspondent alleged, who were the most appreciative fans. Some nearby householders, however, objected to the noise and disturbance that was thereby created.

Aberdour House.

Old Norman Church, Aberdour

35. The ruined St. Fillan's Kirk featured in many postcards. After its restoration in 1925-1926, the former parish church (we see here its interior beneath) was converted into the kirk hall. While staying in the village, many visitors attended one of the local kirks.

Aberdour House also featured in many postcards. In this 1920s view (above), we see a tennis court in the area of the new Earls Gate housing development. During the First World War this former residence of the Morton family was occupied by the dashing Admiral Beatty, who commanded the Rosyth-based battle-cruiser squadron and latterly the entire British Grand Fleet.

Parish Church, Aberdour

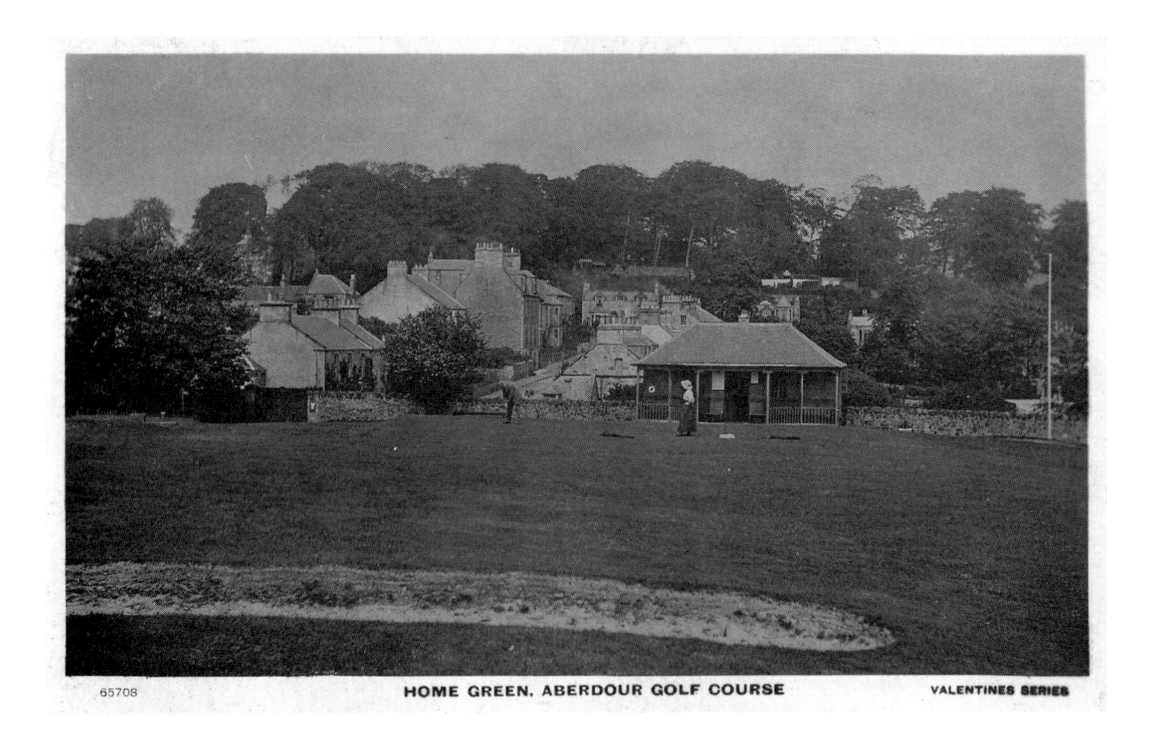

65708
HOME GREEN, ABERDOUR GOLF COURSE
VALENTINES SERIES

36. Turn-of-the-century Aberdour's proud, new amenities included: a public park, a bowling-green, which in 1912 was in a terrible condition (some bowlers played in hob-nailed boots) and a golf-course, created in 1905 'after a friendly negotiation with the Hon. W.C. Hewitt, the Commissioner for the Earl of Moray'. Extended to 18 holes in 1912, the annual subscription, circa 1922, for adult, male golfers was £1: 10 shillings.

37. After the First World War, the Galloway Saloon Steam Packet Company was wound up. Although motor-buses were stiff competitors, some Forth sailings were maintained. In the years 1927 to 1939, the 'Fair Maid' (a former Clyde paddle-steamer) carried on the traditional sailings from Leith to Aberdour and under the Forth Railway Bridge. When war broke out again in September 1939, the 'Fair Maid' left Aberdour for the last time, her orchestra playing 'Polly-Wolly-Doodle, Fare thee well, Fare thee well.'

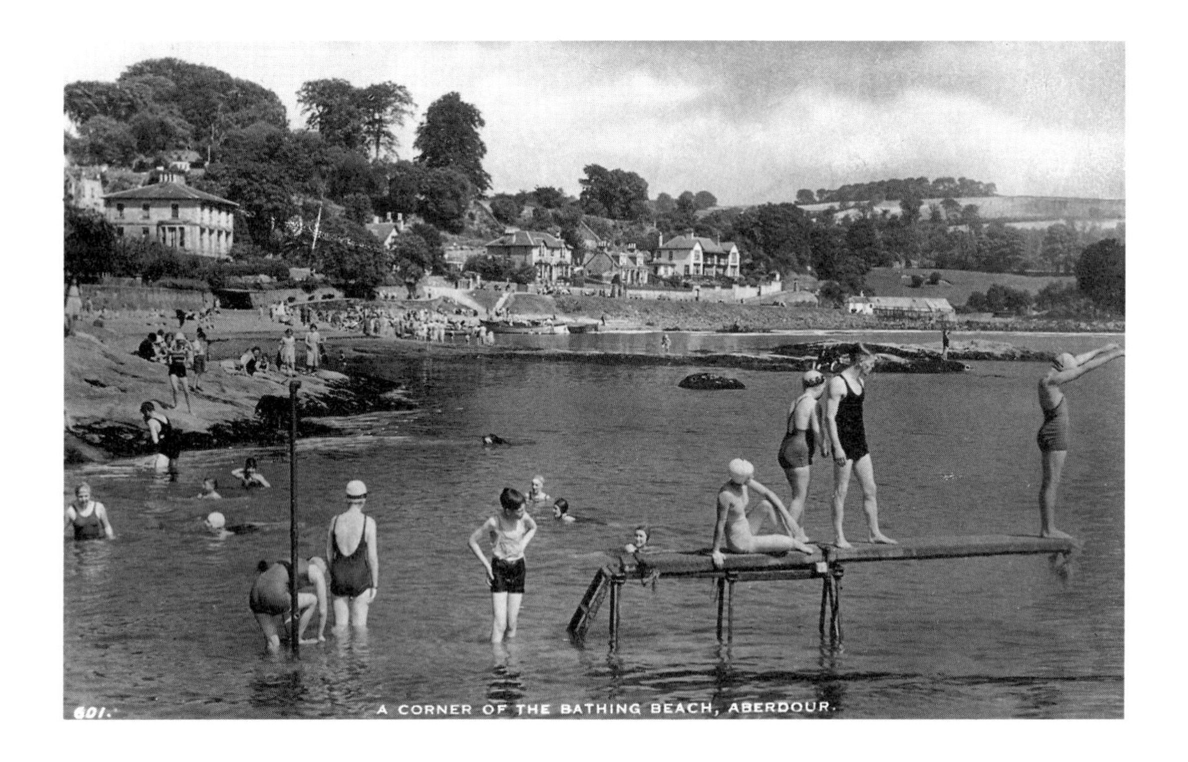

38. While the 'Fair Maid' did not come back to the Forth after the war, the crowds did return to their old seaside haunts. Postcards were in short supply, though. In the era of wartime shortages and post-war austerity, few new ones were available and old stock like this fine mid-1930s card (issued by J.B. White Ltd. of Dundee) was still being sold. The May 1945 postmark on the card included Victory Bells to celebrate Victory in Europe. The sender had been spending her VE holiday weekend in Aberdour. Today the crowds depart for warmer climes and all that remains of the diving board are some bits of rusted stanchion.

HIGH STREET AND HARBOUR PLACE, BURNTISLAND.
Published by Andrew Young, Burntisland.

39. Coming now to Burntisland, we start with an old view of the High Street and Harbour Place, which were the focal points for the burgh's trade and commerce. The baskets and barrels in the left-hand corner remind us of the town's past as a fishing port. Sailing ships came very close to Harbour Place or The Shore, as it used to be termed.

40. The number of inns, hotels, ship's chandlers and a shipsmith confirm the importance of Harbour Place to the maritime community. The George Hotel is now the Smugglers' Inn, but the Harbour Inn next door is gone. Behind and above it stood the Seamen's Lodging House. Round the corner, the Forth Hotel was handy for rail travellers going to or from the ferry. Because of the ferry to Granton, Burntisland was the principal entry point for travellers coming from the south. James Louden ran the hotel from 1903 to 1914. Latterly, the building was used as railway company offices.

41. When this card was posted in 1907, through trains were coming to Burntisland from the west via the Forth Bridge. The new platforms and ticket offices, which were built to cater for this traffic, are shown in this early 20th century photograph. Improved communication with the west was offset by the drastic decline in ferry traffic for both passengers and coal.

42. Prior to 1890, coal from Fife was shipped across the Forth, using roll-on roll-off ferry boats. Inaugurated in 1850, this was the world's first ro-ro ferry. In this 1888 picture, the vessel being loaded at the adjustable ramp is the North British Railway Company's twin-funnel paddler 'Midlothian'. The paddle-steamer on the right is a passenger-carrying ferryboat, the Kinghorn-built 'John Stirling'.

43. Although ferry traffic declined after 1890, the railway company-owned paddle-steamer, the 'William Muir', maintained a regular service from Granton to Burntisland until it was scrapped in 1937. In 1910, the 'Willie Muir', as it was more generally called, underwent a major refit and was left with only one funnel instead of the two shown here. In 1906, when this card was posted, the East Dock was comparatively new. The lock gates which gave entrance to the new dock are on the right.

THE DOCKS, BURNTISLAND.
Published by Andrew Young, Burntisland.

44. We now look across the West Dock towards the harbour entrance. As well as steamboats, several sailing ships are visible in this turn-of-the-century photograph. Harbour Place, with the Forth Hotel (a rear view), is in the top left-hand corner, with the Engine House, with its smokestack, just to the right. The East Dock lies beyond.

45. North British and Fife Coal Company railway waggons, sidings, coal-hoists and steam-ships were part-and-parcel of the harbour scene. The docks, which were developed and expanded between 1876 and 1902, provided work for railway workers, dockers, coal-trimmers, pilots and other boatmen. The construction, from the 1880s, and subsequent extension of Methil Docks, however, brought into being a serious competitor. This and other factors meant that the population of Burntisland declined between 1901 and 1911.

46. In this pre-1922 view of the West Dock, we are looking towards Rossend Castle and the Burntisland Oil Mill, the building with the big lum on the right. Following the opening of the new dock in 1876, this former Sugar House was adapted for seed-crushing, the end-products being linseed and cotton-seed animal feeding stuffs and cotton-seed oil, which went to make margarine. This building was demolished in 1970.

47. In this aerial view we see Burntisland Shipyard (opened in 1918), with two vessels under construction. The founders, the Ayre brothers, were pioneers in prefabrication. Between 1918 and 1968 over 420 ships were constructed at the yard. As for the port, apart from one vessel in the East Dock and another at the Ferry Pier, it is virtually empty. Tied up at the Ferry Pier, we see the 'Willie Muir', which by that time had just a single funnel.

48. The shipyard had a vital role to play during the Second World War, including designing and building dual-purpose vessels like the 'Empire MacKendrick'. Designed to transport bulk grain across the Atlantic, this 8,345 ton ship, which was launched in 1943, also served as an aircraft-carrier. The planes flying from merchant aircraft-carriers like this, helped to protect wartime convoys from attacks by German U-boats. Observe the suction pipe for loading and discharging grain.

49. After the war, the Burntisland shipyard launched many fine ships, including (left) the 'Dispatcher', an early 1950s bauxite carrier. This 8,000 ton vessel was built for the ALCOA Steamship Company of the U.S.A. A wide sweep of the town is shown in the other mid-1950s photographs, which were taken from a shipyard crane. The flag-adorned M.V. 'Huntsfield' (top picture) was an 11,000 ton vessel, built for London owners. This ship, or a sister vessel, appears in the lower picture behind the 'Capetan Chiotis', the ship being pulled by a tugboat.

50. The coming of the railway heralded a new age of prosperity for Victorian Burntisland. The North British Railway Company built, repaired and fitted engines, waggons and carriages at its Burntisland depot, which was centred on the Round House. The photograph was taken circa 1935, prior to the demolition of this massive, and appropriately-named, structure.

51. The British Aluminium Company's works (since 1982, ALCAN) is seen here from the south. Initially, there was considerable local opposition to its construction, with many locals dreading the impact of the aluminium works on Burntisland's reputation as a holiday resort. In this 1920s view we see, on the extreme left, the Newbigging railway signal box and the old low-level water cooler, with steam billowing forth.

The Sea Mill. Burntisland.
One of the "Seven Wonders of Fife".
The wheels are turned by the incoming and outgoing tides.
J. R. R. — E.

52. The Sea Mill, here described as one of the 'Seven Wonders of Fife', was driven by seawater. Water from the incoming tide was trapped by the wall shown on the right, and then used to drive the mill's undershot water-wheel. In this south-looking photograph (postmark date 1907), we see the mill 'pond', the mill buildings (part of which survives) and, behind, West Broom Hill. This view obviously predates the construction of the Rossend Castle housing estate.

53. Historic Rossend Castle, here shown from the harbour, became a boarding house. In the early, pioneering days of the Burntisland Shipyard, Wilfrid Ayre, who was later knighted, used Rossend as his headquarters' office. After two public enquiries, Rossend Castle was saved from demolition and in 1975 was converted into an architects' office by the Hurd Rolland partnership.

54. Looking north towards Braehead and Kirkton, we see Ged's Mill with its prominent smokestack and, in the distance, the Grange Distillery (now containing bonded warehouses), which distilled Old Burntisland whisky until circa 1920. The aluminium works now occupy much of the former Ged's Mill site. From that complex of buildings only the doocot, to the left of the big chimney, is still visible. Streets of houses now fill the fields, which, around 1900, were still farmland.

55. To move goods around in Edwardian Burntisland, you used hand-carts and horse-drawn vehicles, but observe too in this High Street scene the lad with the box on his head. The curious shop-sign on the left looks like a lifebelt. The shop was a ship chandler's – one of four which sold marine equipment and ship's supplies. Further along, on the same side of the street, is the Star Inn, which now has two gables facing the High Street, then only one.

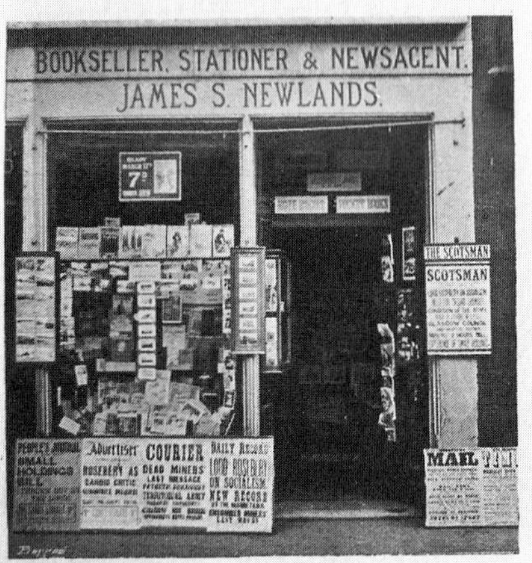

James S. Newlands

BOOKSELLER STATIONER and NEWSPAPER AGENT,

72, High Street,

OPPOSITE KIRKGATE. **Burntisland.**

PICTORIAL POST-CARDS.
LOCAL and OTHER VIEWS, Etc.

GOLF CLUBS AND BALLS.

Daily and Weekly Newspapers promptly delivered Morning and : : : : Evening. : : : :

CHEAP BOOKS, CREST CHINA, MAGAZINES, PERIODICALS

56. The building on the corner, where Lothian Street leaves the High Street, is gone. Alex. Thomson, baker and confectioner, had the corner shop. Further along the High Street, we see that James S. Newlands believed in the power of advertisement, showing his wares in every possible space, both inside and outside the shop. By selling postcards, crested china, golf clubs and balls, he catered for visitors' needs.

Burntisland. The High Street. This is the best business part of the town, and consists
of a wide, spacious thoroughfare leading to the Links and the Sands.

57. As we observe in this circa 1900 High Street scene (above), boys either wore tackety boots or went barefoot. The Auld Free Kirk on the right, next to the toon hoose, was knocked down to make way for the new Carnegie Library, shown in the other picture. Notice the top-hatted notabilities and police surrounding Andrew Carnegie, who on that same day was given the freedom of the burgh. In the same year, 1907, that Burntisland library was opened, the corner-stone for the Hague Peace Palace was laid – another edifice that the Scottish-American billionaire paid for.

58. The town house and library appear again in this splendid photograph, depicting a couple, probably the owners, at the door of the Commercial Restaurant. The window display includes tempting-looking sponge-cakes and glass-stoppered jars, filled with biscuits. Pratt, the china merchant next door, displays souvenir plates, a popular purchase with holiday-makers.

59. Looking down the Kirkgate in the 1920s, we see dwellings that have now gone and observe that, in the middle distance, there were then only two houses on Broomhill Road, both Pilkington-designed. What are the girls in the right-hand corner up to? Only the barefoot girl on the left seems to have noticed the photographer. By the 1920s, though, cameras were much smaller and less obtrusive. The earlier photographers with their plate cameras and tripods were much more noticeable.

60. A delivery cart, bearing milk-churns, is prominent in this pre-1908 scene. The photographer was looking east, along Leven Street, towards Thistle Cottage on the right. In the summer of 1993, the further-away tenement blocks were standing empty. After the First World War the tenement-style building, so favoured by Victorian and Edwardian builders, went out of fashion.

61. The children in this circa 1937 picture were photographed in front of a recently demolished house in Somerville Street. The pistol-packing lad on the left is wearing a Boys Brigade belt and pouch. A couple of shipyard apprentices, standing at the back, have joined the group.

62. Returning to the High Street, we observe in this 1935-dated postcard, that the Burntisland Co-op was a very important retail operator, but that there were plenty of small shops catering for locals and visitors alike. By then, many visitors possessed cameras and would have availed themselves of the 'Films Developed' service. While motor vehicles were more prominent, there were still quite a few horse-drawn carts on the streets. Thus, the horse trough (with ornamental lamp) on the left was still regarded as a useful piece of street furniture.

63. Looking from the links towards the East Port, we note that the children in the foreground are spread out, almost certainly deliberately posed by the photographer. While the corner buildings have not changed much, the entrance to the links has been transformed, since this turn-of-the-century photo was taken. New public toilets now provide a necessary adjunct to the fine Victorian drinking fountain, recently flitted to this spot. The fountain originally stood at the Craigholm Crescent corner.

64. Early in the 20th century, as now, the links were used for many different forms of leisure. In this picture we see a well-attended cricket match with sight screens at each end of the pitch and tents, which were presumably used for 'changing-rooms' and for serving teas during the interval. Golf, too, was once played there. A plan of 1813 shows 4 golf holes marked out on the links.

BURNTISLAND FROM THE DELVES.
Published by Andrew Young, Burntisland.
To wish you Many happy returns of the day
Jan 9th 1903.

65. The links and the Round House too (far left) appear in the postcard of Burntisland from the Delves. As the empty fields in the foreground and elsewhere show, the Burntisland of 1903, when this card was posted, was more compact, and much more crowded, than it is today. The row of stacks in the foreground indicates, too, that the harvest was in. Kirkbank Road is on the right and Kinghorn Road on the left. The Bentfield Villas, with their flat-topped roofs (left), were designed in this way, we are told, so as not to obstruct the view from Greenmount House.

66. Looking towards the beach from the Lammerlaws, we see part of the New Town. The cannon (bottom left) was used for practice by the local Artillery Volunteers. The Volunteers' Battery and Drill Ground was adjacent to a row of fishermen's cottages. Notice the boats drawn up on the shore. Although the card is dated 1904, the photograph must have been taken prior to 1903, since the Erskine United Free Kirk is not shown.

67. Now we see the Erskine Kirk, which was completed in 1903. The church, where this congregation had formerly worshipped, stood on the High Street (see No. 57). When it was demolished, the site was used for the new Carnegie Library. A group of children, including some youthful gowfers, pose for the camera. The barefooted bairns were not necessarily impoverished.

68. The death of George Ferguson in 1901, the Fife Free Press stated, 'removes from the town a very enterprising builder, who for a period of 40 years, has had the chief hand in its extensions... Ferguson Place and Ferguson Square bear his name.' On the left we see the school erected by the Burntisland School Board in 1876. James Lothian Mitchell was headmaster from 1892 until his dismissal in 1906, the result of local political machinations.

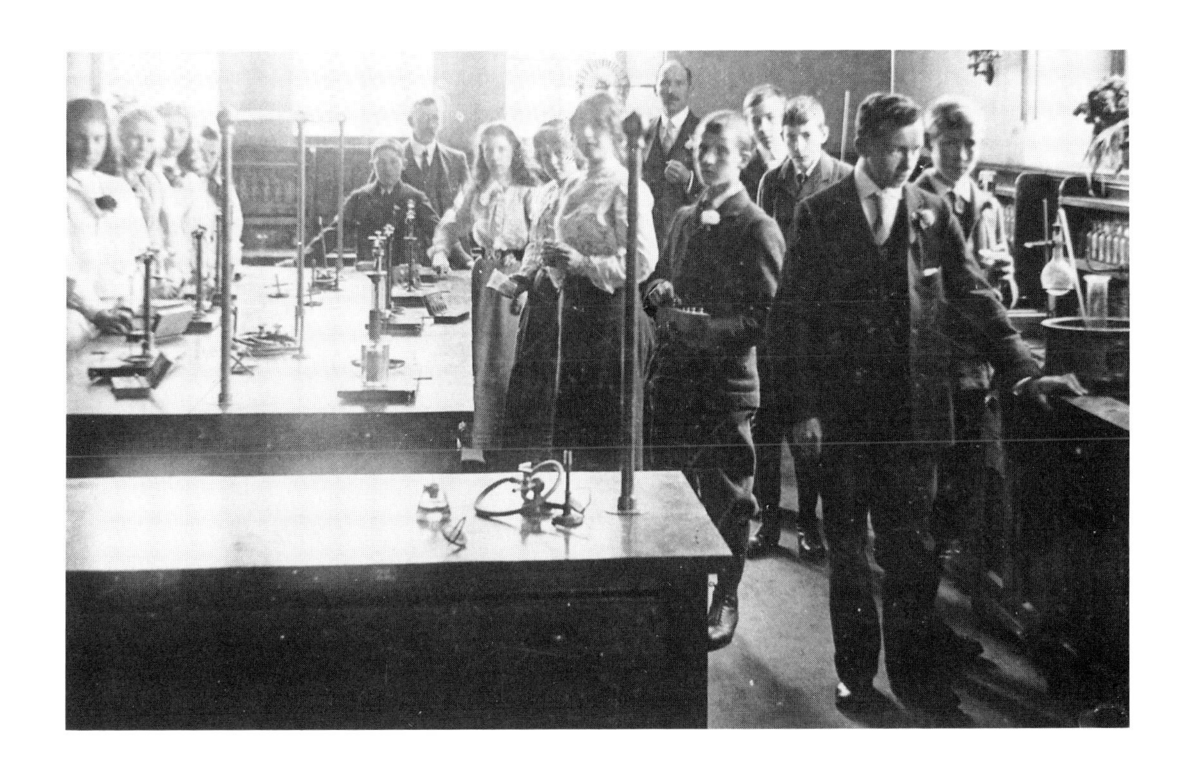

69. James Lothian appears at the back of this circa 1901 photograph of the school science laboratory. During his time at Burntisland, Mitchell, a very enterprising teacher, introduced a secondary department which, with the construction next door of a new building, became a Higher Grade School. Mitchell was a prominent figure in the town council and other local organisations.

70. Boat trips, sand and sea attracted crowds to the beach, although the coats, jackets and woolly jumpers indicate that the weather was not too warm. Some children are paddling, but very few bathing costumes are being worn. Very few people possessed special beach or leisure wear. In the distance we see the beach shelter, the tearoom (converted out of a former bathing house) and beyond, another older seawater bath house (now a dwelling-place). The promenade was extended to the Lochies in 1905.

71. Again, sensible warm garments are the rule in this beach scene. With three policemen to keep control, Edwardian sandcastle contests must have been highly competitive. The policeman on the left must have cracked a joke, as the spectators in his immediate vicinity are looking admiringly in his direction, whereas most of the rest are looking towards the camera. Some of the boys are wearing blazers, caps and identical ties, and one at least a football shirt.

72. This souvenir card of Dalton Payne's Entertainers shows what smart men and women were wearing in 1923. This was one of the many troupes that spent a summer season at Burntisland. Before and during the First World War, Fred Collins' pierrot troupe played at Burntisland in successive seasons. More active forms of recreation included bowling and tennis, played at, for instance, the Recreation Grounds, which were run by a private company.

73. Constructed by Burntisland Town Council at a cost of £10,000, the bathing pool was opened in June 1936 and was immediately highly popular. In the first season, when this card was posted, there was no tearoom. It was a later addition. Closed at the end of the 1978 season, Kirkcaldy District Council announced in April 1979 that the pool was to be permanently closed. A council promise, made later that year, that a new indoor pool would be erected, was not implemented. In 1990, the derelict pool was demolished and the site landscaped.

74. An earlier open-air swimming pond was constructed, circa 1906, on the eastern side of the Lammerlaws, an area which, as this early 1930s card shows, was popular for boating as well as for bathing. The grassy area above the promenade was, we see, a favourite site for campers. The ruins of the former vitriol works are on the left.

75. East of Burntisland lay the Binn Village, built to accommodate Binnend Oil Company employees and their families. Inaugurated in 1878, this company produced shale-oil and byproducts until 1892, when it collapsed and was liquidated. The huge bing behind overshadowed the set of goal-posts beside the school, which was on the extreme left. The oil-works lay out of sight on the lower ground to the right. This card was posted in 1907 when all workers had gone, but the Binnend cottages provided cheap lodgings for holiday-makers coming across the Firth from Edinburgh and Leith.

76. We conclude with a photograph of the Armistice Day parade in November 1947, when local organisations marched along the High Street to the War Memorial to pay their respects to those who sacrificed their lives in the two World Wars. The group abreast of Porte House comprises the members of Rossend Chapter 409 Burntisland Eastern Star. The frontages seen here, have been greatly altered. There is still, though, a Co-op, although now shifted slightly to the right, much reduced in size, and, like so many other shops and premises in both Burntisland and Aberdour, under different management.